Haiti: The Enduring Spirit of a Nation

Philip Mshelia
Haiti: The Enduring Spirit of a Nation

—

Published by - Spines
ISBN: 979-8-89569-107-6

Haiti: The Enduring Spirit of a Nation

Heralding the season of Peace and Prosperity

Philip Mshelia

Contents

About the Book

Do not dismiss this book simply because it centers on Haiti. Within its pages lies the potential to profoundly transform your understanding of nation-building, self-worth, and the power of human resilience. This work serves as a vital resource for anyone seeking enlightenment and purpose, regardless of their background or beliefs. Crafted for those who value progress and empowerment, it inspires readers to recognize their intrinsic worth and contribute meaningfully to their community's vision.

Despite the formidable crises Haiti faces—poverty, instability, and deep-rooted challenges—this book offers a perspective that is both transformative and hopeful. It reveals how, even in the most difficult circumstances, extraordinary change is not only possible but within reach. It demonstrates that people of value are the strength of a nation, and when those individuals are uplifted, the entire nation flourishes.

More than a reflection on Haiti's journey, this book is a manifesto of hope, resilience, and transformation—an invitation for every reader to recognize their power to change not only their own lives but the destiny of their communities and nations. It reaffirms Haiti's potential and its vital role as a source of inspiration and transformation, proving that even in the face of overwhelming challenges, a brighter future is always within reach.

For the Unsung Heroes of Haiti

Dedicated to those who champion peace, to those who imagine a brighter future, and to those who rise above their struggles—your impact is profound, and your story is the soul of this book.

About the Author

Philip W. Mshelia is an author, speaker, educator, and veterinary expert specializing in equine medicine. He founded the Kingdom Mindset, a pioneering mentorship program that empowers young people to actively contribute to economic development and nation-building. He is also the co-founder of Hope Interactive, extending his influence beyond his profession by focusing on charitable and social causes.

Philip's diverse interests span literature, equine care, and music composition. His passion for writing is evident in his book *Unraveling the Mystery of Songwriting* and his contributions to several scholarly works. He is currently working on new titles, including *Africa: Return to the Path of Honor*, *Aligning with the Revelation of the Season*, and *Redefining Leadership in Africa*, reflecting his commitment to intellectual growth and a Kingdom-centered worldview. Through his work, Philip W. Mshelia emerges as a promising voice in education, mentorship, and societal development.

INTRODUCTION

Haiti, the first independent nation in Latin America and the Caribbean, boldly secured its freedom from France in 1804 through a remarkable slave revolt led by visionary leaders like Toussaint Louverture and Jean-Jacques Dessalines. This historic victory was more than the birth of a nation—it was a powerful declaration against colonial oppression, a symbol of resilience that reverberated across the world.

Yet despite its courageous beginnings, Haiti has faced profound and enduring challenges, marred by government corruption, incompetence, and the dominance of a privileged few. Corruption has not only weakened the nation's economic and social stability but has also obstructed its pursuit of lasting prosperity. Haiti's vibrant culture, deeply rooted in the syncretic religion of voodoo—a fusion of African, indigenous, and Christian traditions—continues to shape its spiritual and cultural identity, for better and for worse.

The world shares a collective hope for a peaceful and stable Haiti, one that demands a collaborative approach—uniting both internal strength and external support to confront the nation's deep-rooted issues. For Haiti to transcend its current struggles and emerge stronger, it must reconnect with the divine revelations and historical wisdom that once fueled its rise.

True leadership is forged in moments of profound clarity and understanding. Visionary leadership—anchored in deep insight and spiritual discernment—has the transformative power to uplift a nation and guide it toward renewal. Haiti's rich history and the unyielding spirit of its people hold the keys to unlocking this potential, provided they are led by those who can see beyond the present challenges.

However, this battle is not merely political or social; it is also spiritual. A shadow of deception and manipulation—symbolized by the influence of Jezebel—clouds the nation's ability to discern truth from falsehood, light from darkness. This spiritual blindness threatens to stifle Haiti's potential to embrace its divine destiny.

Yet there is hope. Just as Jesus brought light to Galilee, illuminating a path to transformation, so too can Haiti find its way to peace and restoration. The dawn of healing begins with a return to foundational values, as the Sun of Righteousness rises, ushering in a new era of honor and resilience. Haiti's past is not merely a tale of struggle; it is a wellspring of lessons that can lead to greatness. By realigning with its core values and divine insights, Haiti has the opportunity to redefine its narrative and stand as a beacon of hope and integrity for the world.

The journey to renewal is not just a possibility—it is a calling waiting to be answered. Haiti's future, shaped by its rich history and guided by its untapped potential, beckons for leaders who can see beyond the immediate and inspire a nation to reach for the extraordinary. The path to greatness lies ahead, and Haiti is poised to seize its rightful place as a symbol of hope, resilience, and transformation.

Let There Be Peace

"Make the habit of two things - to help, or at least, to do no harm."

-Hippocrates

The world's collective heartbeat echoes with a shared dream: peace and stability for Haiti. This is more than just an aspiration—it is a calling that stirs the conscience of all who yearn for justice and prosperity. Transforming this dream into reality demands far more than hope. It requires united efforts—Haitians and the international community standing shoulder to shoulder—to confront the deep-rooted causes of conflict, fostering genuine unity and reconciliation.

To be your brother's or sister's keeper is not just an ancient proverb; it is a rallying call to action. It means standing beside others in their times of need, shielding them from harm, advocating on their behalf, and providing the resources they need to succeed. It is about leading by example—embodying integrity and guiding others toward wise and courageous decisions.

By embracing this spirit of solidarity, we can ignite meaningful change. Together, we can transform shared hopes into lasting realities—not just for Haiti, but for communities around the world. This is the essence of peacemaking: creating the fertile soil in which hope, growth, and prosperity can take root and flourish.

People can live in peace by respecting each other's beliefs, values, and opinions. Peace requires us to listen, to seek understanding, and to embrace the beauty of diversity. By being tolerant, accepting differences in culture, religion, and lifestyle, and working together to resolve conflicts, we pave the way to a brighter future. As it is written, "Blessed are the peacemakers, for they shall be called sons of God" (Matthew 5:9, ESV).

A peaceful nation creates an atmosphere ripe for development. When a country experiences peace, it can channel its resources, efforts, and energy into progress—economic, social, and cultural. Peace is the bedrock of development; it provides a stable and secure environment where citizens can live without fear, enabling them to engage in productive activities, invest in businesses, and pursue education—all of which contribute to national prosperity.

Peace attracts investment. Domestic and foreign investors are far more likely to invest in a nation that offers stability and security. Such investments lead to job creation, improved infrastructure, and increased economic growth, ultimately benefiting the entire nation. Moreover, peace fosters social cohesion and unity among different communities and groups. In a peaceful society, people are more likely to work together, pursue common goals, and create social programs that benefit all.

Peace also encourages innovation and creativity. When individuals are not consumed by fear or insecurity, they can focus on generating new ideas, developing technologies, and finding innovative solutions to the challenges they face. This spirit of creativity drives development in every sector of society.

A peaceful nation also opens doors to international cooperation. Diplomatic relations, global trade, and cultural exchange flourish where peace reigns, contributing to technological advancements and economic prosperity. Ultimately, peace allows individuals to live lives free from violence, discrimination, and oppression

—empowering them to grow, develop, and fulfill their potential, contributing to their nation's strength.

However, peace is more than the absence of conflict—it embodies justice, equality, and respect for human rights. True peace is built on a foundation of social and economic equity, inclusivity, and the fair treatment of all citizens. Only when these principles are upheld can a nation truly unlock its full potential, paving the way for prosperity and an improved quality of life for all.

Healing Begins with Us

Haiti already possesses the seeds of peace that she seeks. Healing has begun as the Sun of Righteousness rises over her. The lessons from Haiti's history are not chains that bind; rather, they are keys that unlock resilience and honor. Haiti's story is one of courage—a story that has endured slavery, revolutions, and countless hardships. It is time to reclaim that history, to realign, and to rewrite the narrative. As promised in Scripture: "And I will give peace in the land, and ye shall lie down, and none shall make you afraid: and I will rid evil beasts out of the land, neither shall the sword go through your land" (Leviticus 26:6, KJV).

God hears the cries of His people. "The LORD hears his people when they call to him for help. He rescues them from all their troubles. The LORD is close to the brokenhearted; he rescues those whose spirits are crushed" (Psalm 34:17-18, NLT). Haiti, this promise is for you. The time has come to transform despair into hope and to let the spirit of peace lead you forward. As Isaiah declares, "Violence shall no more be heard in thy land, wasting nor destruction within thy borders; but thou shalt call thy walls Salvation, and thy gates Praise" (Isaiah 60:18, KJV).

The gates to peace and prosperity are wide open. This transformation does not require wealth or power; it only requires the commitment of those who have discovered the value of life and are ready to live by it.

. . .

Haiti Needs Peacemakers

Haiti is wounded, and what she needs most is peaceful people—those who are willing to bring healing and hope. It is these individuals who will "salt" Haiti, preserving its essence and bringing out its best. Jesus came to offer the earth what it lacked, while Satan's purpose was to kill, steal, and destroy. The Spirit of Christ is a life-giving force, and those who possess this life should be a source of restoration, not destruction. As Rev. Chris Christian rightly says, "Men resort to violence when they are devalued." Therefore, the path to peace begins with restoring the inherent value of every Haitian.

Haiti needs peacemakers—those who can contribute to the nation's peace, unity, and progress. Political instability and social unrest have left the country scarred, with fragile governance and inadequate infrastructure. In such circumstances, peaceful people have the power to foster dialogue, reconciliation, and understanding. They can act as bridge-builders between divided factions and work toward the common good.

The economic challenges Haiti faces are pressing. Ranked among the poorest countries in the Western Hemisphere, Haiti struggles with high rates of unemployment, poverty, and inequality. Peaceful actors have a critical role in promoting an environment conducive to investment, entrepreneurship, and sustainable development. Their efforts can improve Haiti's economic prospects and uplift communities across the nation.

Beyond economics, Haiti's very identity depends on social cohesion. Peaceful contributors—those who serve as cultural ambassadors, advocates for justice, and bridge-builders—can help create a more harmonious and inclusive society. Haiti needs these people to thrive. Their commitment to peace, dialogue, and cooperation can build a more stable, prosperous, and cohesive nation, for the benefit of all Haitians.

. . .

A Vision for a Transformed Haiti

The dawn of peace in Haiti begins with each one of us answering the call to be peacemakers. It begins with seeing beyond our differences and embracing our common humanity. Haiti's potential is limitless, but this potential can only be unlocked through unity, justice, and a shared commitment to building a future that honors the sacrifices of the past.

The road to peace is not easy, but it is a journey worth taking—a journey that promises healing, renewal, and transformation. Haiti can rise to her true destiny, but it requires us to be more than observers. It calls us to action—to be agents of peace, sowers of hope, and builders of a future worthy of the resilience and courage that define the Haitian spirit.

Let there be peace. Not a peace that is merely the absence of conflict, but a transformative peace that brings justice, prosperity, and the fulfillment of every dream that Haiti's people hold in their hearts. This is the peace we seek, and this is the peace we must create.

Declare Your Season: Haiti's Divine Awakening

"Declare your season, for in understanding life's rhythms, you unlock the power to transform challenges into growth, embrace change with courage, and thrive in every chapter of your journey."

– Philip Mshelia

To secure true freedom and cast-off manipulation, Haiti must find refuge in the divine revelations that brought her into being. A nation's strength, its very heartbeat, lies in knowing its identity—rooted in revelation. Haiti must awaken to the truth of what gave her life if she is to flourish in this new season. Even a subdued nation can rise to greatness through the power of discovery, vision, and reclaiming its true identity. The true destiny of Haiti is buried within the revelation that birthed her, waiting for her people to uncover it.

As Mike Murdock once said, "The difference in seasons is who you choose to believe." God tabernacles within a nation, ready to share His destiny, but so too does the enemy of all goodness. When the devil seeks to destroy, he sends messengers of darkness to obscure truth and veil hope. When God wants to bless a nation, He sends torchbearers—messengers of revelation and light.

The devil's mission is simple: to blind people from their true freedom. He casts a shadow of confusion and limits understanding, ensuring that people never value their spiritual eyes. He tirelessly fights against vision, knowing full well that vision births freedom, salvation, and dominion. The system of many nations is built on lies designed to keep the people bound in darkness. But there is an undeniable truth—light dispels darkness. Haiti must declare her season and uncover the divine revelation that brings her to the light.

Seeking Preservation, Finding Greatness

A preserved nation cannot be denied its rightful place among great nations. However, any country that glorifies death or bears the mark of decay will destroy itself from within. Haiti must build a generation that is anchored in divine wisdom and filled with spiritual strength. To fight devaluation, the nation must focus on the truth of God's Word, discern His heart, and cleanse its firmament from the distortions of darkness.

Revelation and truth are at the core of every nation's journey. "The mysteries of a season connect people to the ruling spirit of that season," says Rev. Chris Christian. To confront the challenges of today, the revelations of God concerning Haiti must become her refuge and rallying call, empowering her people to stand unshaken in their identity and destiny.

Breaking the Chains of Enslavement

Enslaving a nation, stripping it of resources, and subduing its spirit is a great evil, but divine justice prevails over any plot of darkness. As it is written, "There is no wisdom, no insight, no plan that can succeed against the Lord" (Proverbs 21:30, NLT). God declares, "I am the Lord, the God of all the peoples of the world. Is anything too hard for me?" (Jeremiah 32:27, NLT). Even in seasons of hardship, divine power endures, and the promise of God cannot be silenced.

For Haiti to experience true transformation, her seers, visionaries, and leaders must rise and declare this new season. It is not God alone who declares a season—He partners with humanity. Just as Adam named the animals in Eden, Haiti's people must call forth their new destiny. The earth and its fullness belong to God, but it is given to humanity to establish His will. In Haiti's declaration, the power of God will manifest, and in this divine partnership, a renewed Haiti shall emerge.

The Wisdom of the Issacharites: Understanding the Times

The Bible tells of the children of Issachar, who understood the times and knew what Israel should do (1 Chronicles 12:32). This wisdom allowed them to provide guidance during critical moments of change. Similarly, Haiti's leaders must embrace this legacy, gaining insight into the complexities of today and guiding the nation toward divine alignment. By integrating divine wisdom, Haiti can rise above confusion and move forward with clarity and purpose, turning current challenges into steppingstones to greatness.

When a nation fails to declare its season, it remains trapped, serving the interests of adversaries. But when visionaries rise, they shape the era, declare their beliefs, and invite divine power into their midst. Haiti must nurture leaders who will stand with boldness and declare a new season—one of resilience, stability, and hope.

Travail in the Spirit: The Battle for Light

Darkness will continue its grip until people of value arise with the light to declare their season. As it says in the Word, "His life brought light to everyone... and the light shines in the darkness" (John 1:4). The battle against darkness is not fought by prayer alone

—it is won as individuals progressively bring forth the light needed to claim their season.

Whenever God desires to accomplish His purpose, He awaits a willing and obedient vessel. The responsibility of what unfolds on earth lies with humanity, and the presence of people of value is a sign of God's favor upon that time.

The Voice of God in the Seasons

Every season—whether of prosperity or adversity, transition or triumph—carries its own "cloud of witnesses." These witnesses are active participants in the unfolding divine narrative. God speaks through each season, and His presence is undeniable. As Ecclesiastes 3:1 says, "To everything there is a season, a time for every purpose under heaven."

In every moment, God is open to conversation with His people. His voice called to Moses in the burning bush, and Jesus taught the multitudes in His time. "My sheep hear my voice, and I know them, and they follow me" (John 10:27). In every season, God speaks; those attuned to His voice hear His call.

Declaring Haiti's New Era

God's voice is present in every season, guiding His people through the uncertainties of life. His promise is clear: "Whether you turn to the right or to the left, your ears will hear a voice behind you, saying, 'This is the way; walk in it'" (Isaiah 30:21). It is up to us to respond—to declare our season and act in alignment with His guidance.

Haiti's moment is now. Let this be the season of declaring a new era, with seers and seekers rising, guided by God's voice, and setting the nation on a path of lasting hope, peace, and prosperity.

Building a Nation Rooted in Value

"As you become more aware of the world within you, your presence in the outside world becomes more meaningful."

-Bhawna Gautam

A nation's greatness is not measured by its wealth but by the value of its people. The strength of a nation lies in individuals who possess intrinsic worth and purpose—people whose lives contribute to the well-being and progress of society. When these individuals depart, they take with them the essence that holds the nation together, leaving behind a barren land devoid of life and vitality. As it is written in **Proverbs 29:18 (KJV)**, "Where there is no vision, the people perish." Without people of value, a nation's future becomes bleak, and its potential is stifled.

Human beings are divine gateways to the earth, chosen by God to manifest His eternal purposes. Whenever God seeks to intervene in the affairs of this world, He looks for willing vessels—people of value who can carry out His will. Nations that devalue human life and waste the potential of their people rarely rise to prominence. They sabotage their destinies, killing the custodians of their liberty. As **Ephesians 4:17-19 (NIV)** warns, living without purpose leads to futility, emphasizing the necessity of walking in the light of understanding and truth.

Rediscovering a Nation's True Worth

The revival of a broken nation begins when it starts to see itself through the eyes of God. A nation must discover its true identity and recognize the invaluable worth of its citizens. The beauty and strength of a nation are found not in its material wealth but in the collective value of its people. History is shaped by the values that a nation cultivates within its citizens, and from these discovered values, a great nation is born.

Vision is the cornerstone of a nation's strength. Without vision, people are easily manipulated and led astray, becoming tools in the hands of those who seek to exploit them. Visionary individuals possess the profound ability to counteract the forces of darkness. They are the guardians of their nation's destiny, resisting the malevolent forces that seek to corrupt and destroy. Haiti, with its rich history and culture, must preserve its identity and resist the overwhelming tide of malevolence. As **Psalm 127:1 (NIV)** reminds us, "Unless the Lord builds the house, the builders labor in vain." It is the vision and purpose instilled by God that will safeguard a nation's future.

The Sacred Bond Between People and Community

The relationship between people and their community is sacred. It is this bond that sustains a nation and prevents it from falling into chaos. Those who lack purpose contribute to the decay and disintegration of their society. Evil thrives in the hearts of the corrupt, spreading its influence like a plague. True freedom and prosperity cannot flourish among people lost in confusion and chaos. It requires a disciplined, visionary populace that is aware of its inherent value and purpose.

The first strategy of those who seek to manipulate and exploit a weaker nation is to erode the self-worth of its people. They sow seeds of division and self-doubt, creating chaos that allows them to quietly siphon off the nation's resources. Haiti's transformation does not depend on external aid but on rediscovering self-worth and reaffirming its values. As **Proverbs 23:7 (KJV)** states, "For as he thinketh in his heart, so is he." The victory of transformation lies within Haiti's grasp, rooted in the strength of its citizens' values.

Leadership: The Light of a Nation

Leaders are the messiahs of their nations, embodying the essence of guidance and illumination, much like candlesticks lighting the path forward. The ability to lead effectively is not merely a matter of skill; it arises from a deeply intuitive mind, one attuned to the profound depths of knowledge and understanding. When a visionary leader steps forward, they inspire their people, unlocking the potential within them. True leadership is rooted in self-discovery; without understanding oneself, one cannot truly guide others.

The path of a leader is not arbitrary; it is ordained through consecration. Those chosen for this role are protected, their strength hidden within the armor of divine revelation. A leader's words are powerful, shaping their image and value. As **Proverbs 18:21 (NKJV)** declares, "Death and life are in the power of the tongue, and those who love it will eat its fruit." A leader who fails to guard their words and secrets jeopardizes their future and that of their nation.

The journey to honor is singular; a leader does not waver between multiple paths. The greatest gift God bestows upon a nation is the endowment of rich and sanctified thoughts. When God desires to elevate a people, He begins by refining their thinking and aligning their minds with the vision that will lead them to success. From this place of vision, divine thoughts are formed, guiding each step toward fulfillment.

The Emergence of Visionary Leaders

A leader emerges from the shadows when they grasp the revelation of their time. This emergence is often subtle, unnoticed until the moment of manifestation arrives. In the context of Haiti, a messianic star has risen, destined to unseat those who have ruled with treachery. This star floods the sky with brilliant light, signaling the imminent transfer of power. The strongholds of corrupt leaders will crumble, for the scepter belongs to Judah, as **Genesis 49:10 (ESV)** prophesies: "The scepter shall not depart from Judah, nor the ruler's staff from between his feet, until tribute comes to him; and to him shall be the obedience of the peoples."

Haiti is a land of kings and queens, built on the sacrifice of blood, tears, and sweat. This heritage cannot be devalued. The future of Haiti is bright, but it requires leaders who understand their divine purpose and are committed to raising a nation of value. As Russell Bruce wisely noted, "Excellence is never an accident; it is the result of high intention, sincere effort, intelligent direction, skillful execution, and the vision to see obstacles as opportunities."

A Call to Excellence and Self-Discovery

The journey toward national excellence begins with self-discovery. Once a nation and its people recognize their worth, they become unstoppable. **Psalm 37:5 (NIV)** encourages us: "Commit your way to the Lord; trust in Him, and He will do this." What God accomplishes in a person who has discovered their purpose cannot be negated by any force on earth.

Those who have discovered themselves are not swayed by their enemies; their recognition of their worth acts as a natural defense. Whenever a demand is placed on such individuals, human values spring into action spontaneously. Thus, a nation's first line of defense is the values held by its citizens.

Haiti's path to greatness lies in the hands of its people. If they rise with courage and conviction, embracing their God-given purpose, the nation will experience a transformation that the world will marvel at. The time for Haiti to reclaim its destiny is now, and it begins with raising people of value, grounded in vision and purpose.

The Gift of Visionary Leadership: Nurturing and Guiding Citizens for Lasting Impact

A visionary leader's ability to nurture and guide citizens effectively is an invaluable gift that can transform a nation. Visionary leaders are not merely figureheads; they are architects of a better future, guiding their people toward progress with purpose and direction. Such leaders thrive on the virtue within them, leading from a realm of vision that inspires and empowers those they serve.

At the heart of visionary leadership lies the power to inspire. Visionary leaders possess a clear and compelling vision of the future, transcending the ordinary and offering a glimpse of what could be. This ability to inspire is rooted in a deep belief in their vision and an unwavering commitment to bringing it to fruition. When citizens are inspired, they become active participants in the journey toward realizing that vision, contributing their talents and energies to a shared goal.

True leadership is not only about having a dream but also about having the courage to act on that dream and guiding others to do the same. Haiti needs such leaders—leaders who will raise a nation of value, uphold the principles of justice, and lead with integrity. The future belongs to those who understand that true power lies not in wealth or force but in the intrinsic value of each human being.

A History of Struggle and Resilience

Every human being on earth keeps company with a particular past.
You must know the past that keeps company with you.

-Rev Christian

Haiti's history is deeply intertwined with the broader narrative of the African diaspora and the unyielding fight for freedom. The people of Haiti trace their origins to diverse regions across Africa, primarily from West Africa, but also from Central Africa. Many Haitians can trace their ancestral roots back to the former Kingdom of Kongo, Benin, and Togoland, among others. This rich and diverse heritage became the foundation for a nation born out of the ashes of enslavement and colonial oppression—a testament to the indomitable spirit of resilience.

Amidst the turbulence of the French Revolution (1789–1799), a seismic shift occurred in the Caribbean. Enslaved Africans, maroons, and free people of color in Haiti, then known as Saint-Domingue, initiated what would become the Haitian Revolution (1791–1804). This revolution, led by the indomitable Toussaint

Louverture, a former slave who rose to become the first Black general in the French Army, was a defining moment in world history. Louverture's leadership and strategic acumen laid the groundwork for a successful revolt against one of the most powerful colonial empires of the time.

After twelve grueling years of conflict—facing the full might of Napoleon Bonaparte's forces—Louverture's successor, Jean-Jacques Dessalines, led the final charge against the French. On January 1, 1804, Dessalines declared Haiti's sovereignty, marking the birth of the first independent nation in Latin America and the Caribbean, the second republic in the Americas, and the first country in the Western Hemisphere to abolish slavery. Haiti's emergence as the only state established by a successful slave revolt was not just a victory for its people but a beacon of hope for oppressed people everywhere.

The Cost of Independence

Haiti's early years of independence were marked by extraordinary achievements but also by profound challenges. The country, rich in culture and resourcefulness, produced leaders like Alexandre Pétion, Haiti's first president, who sought to chart a course for the fledgling nation. However, the path to stability and prosperity was fraught with obstacles. Following a brief period of division, President Jean-Pierre Boyer successfully united the country, but Haiti's first century of independence was nonetheless plagued by political instability and isolation from the international community.

The international response to Haiti's independence was hostile and punitive. In 1825, French King Charles X demanded that Haiti compensate France for the loss of its colony, imposing a staggering indemnity under the threat of military invasion. Twelve French warships were sent to enforce this demand, effectively blackmailing the young nation into economic submission. This debt, which Haiti only fully repaid in 1947, crippled the country's economy for generations, exemplifying the severe consequences of defying colonial powers.

Haiti's struggle for sovereignty and stability was further compounded by both external and internal forces. The nation's leadership, often drawn from the ranks of former slaves, faced not only the practical challenges of nation-building but also spiritual and moral warfare that comes with the pursuit of true freedom. As the Bible teaches in **Ephesians 6:12 (NIV)**: "For our struggle is not against flesh and blood, but against the rulers, against the authorities, against the powers of this dark world and against the spiritual forces of evil in the heavenly realms." Haiti's experience stands as a testament to this spiritual truth—the fight for freedom inevitably draws the attention of both seen and unseen adversaries.

Haiti in the 21st Century: Trials and Triumphs

In the 21st century, Haiti has continued to grapple with profound challenges. The country has endured political upheavals, including a coup d'état that necessitated United Nations intervention. The catastrophic earthquake of 2010, which claimed the lives of over 250,000 people, was a tragedy of unimaginable proportions. In the aftermath, the nation was further devastated by a cholera outbreak, adding to the suffering of its people.

Haiti's socio-economic landscape remains dire. The economy has been in a state of decline, exacerbated by external pressures, such as the International Monetary Fund's demands to cut fuel subsidies, which sparked widespread protests and civil unrest. The political situation has also deteriorated, leading to the absence of any elected government officials as of February 2023, and Haiti was unfortunately designated a failed state.

Yet, despite these overwhelming challenges, the spirit of Haiti remains unbroken. The words of the Apostle Paul resonate profoundly with Haiti's journey: **2 Corinthians 4:8-9 (NIV)** states, "We are hard pressed on every side, but not crushed; perplexed, but not in despair; persecuted, but not abandoned;

struck down, but not destroyed." This enduring resilience is the hallmark of Haiti—a nation that refuses to bow to adversity, standing firm in the face of trials that would break many others.

Migration: A History of Seeking Freedom

Haiti's history of migration is deeply rooted in the challenges that have shaped the nation's character—poverty, natural disasters, political crises, and insecurity. These forces have continually driven Haitians to seek refuge and opportunity beyond their borders. The assassination of President Jovenel Moïse on July 7, 2021, further exacerbated these challenges, plunging the nation into a power vacuum and intensifying the already pressing need for migration.

Yet, amidst these trials, Haiti's spirit has remained unbroken, as exemplified by the actions and words of its leaders. A remarkable instance of this resilience is found in the actions of President Jean-Pierre Boyer, who, despite Haiti's struggles, reached out in solidarity with the people of Greece during their fight for independence. On January 15, 1822, Boyer penned a letter to the renowned Greek scholar Adamantios Korais, acknowledging Greece's struggle against centuries of despotism and expressing Haiti's deep empathy for their cause.

A Message of Unity and Hope

Boyer's letter is a profound testament to the shared human yearning for freedom. "With great enthusiasm," he wrote, "we learned that Hellas was finally forced to take up arms in order to gain her freedom and the position that she once held among the nations of the world." These words capture the essence of Haiti's own hard-fought liberation from the chains of slavery—a struggle that mirrored the Greek fight for freedom.

Although Haiti, a nation still in the throes of post-revolutionary challenges, could not offer military aid or financial support to Greece, Boyer's letter conveyed something even more profound:

spiritual and moral solidarity. His message transcended material aid; it was a declaration of shared values and mutual respect between two nations born out of the crucible of struggle and sacrifice.

Unmasking Manipulation: Who Benefits from Haiti's Struggles?

Haiti's story is one of resilience and struggle, yet beneath the surface lies a web of manipulation spun by forces that profit from its pain. It is essential to unmask the culprits who derive satisfaction from the suffering of its people—those who revel in chaos and despair. These entities may not reside within Haiti's borders, but their influence is felt in every tear shed and every life lost. This is not merely a tale of Haiti; it is a reflection of a global phenomenon where the powerful exploit the vulnerable, perpetuating cycles of violence and subjugation.

The Bible warns in **Proverbs 22:7 (NIV)**, "The rich rule over the poor, and the borrower is slave to the lender." The relationship between wealthy nations and less developed countries like Haiti is often painted as one of mutual benefit, but beneath this veneer lies a darker reality of exploitation. Wealthier nations extract what they need, leaving behind the dregs of prosperity. This dependency is a chain binding Haiti's economy to the whims of foreign powers.

The Path Forward: Reclaiming Spiritual Dominion

Haiti's struggle is not just a political or economic battle—it is a fight for the soul of the nation. The legacy of Toussaint Louverture, Jean-Jacques Dessalines, and countless others who fought for freedom lives on in the spirit of the Haitian people. The Bible states in **2 Chronicles 16:9 (NIV)**, "For the eyes of the Lord range throughout the earth to strengthen those whose hearts are fully committed to him." God is searching for willing vessels—those who will stand up, fight for the soul of Haiti, and take back spiritual dominion.

The soul of a nation represents a profound arena of spiritual encounter, a battleground where competing forces vie for control and influence. Haiti's path to true liberation lies not merely in political reforms but in embracing the power of revelation and spiritual insight. It requires leaders like the children of Issachar, who had "understanding of the times, to know what Israel ought to do" (**1 Chronicles 12:32**, KJV). Haiti needs seers and seekers who understand the divine season and will declare it boldly.

A Call to Rise and Shine

Haiti, the land of kings and queens, built on sacrifice and resilience, stands at the threshold of a new era. The future of Haiti is bright, but it requires leaders who understand their divine purpose and are committed to raising a nation of value. **Psalm 37:5 (NIV)** encourages us: "Commit your way to the Lord; trust in him, and he will do this." What God accomplishes in a people who have discovered their purpose cannot be negated by any force on earth.

A subdued nation can rise to prominence if it sees itself through the lens of God's word and discovers the true value of its people. There is a certain level of devaluation that a nation will never experience if led by visionary leaders. The beauty and strength of a nation are not in its wealth but in its people. When visionaries lead, wealth and prosperity follow. Haiti is the pride of the Caribbean and an island of kings and queens; a nation built on blood, tears, and sweat that can never remain devalued.

Visionary Leadership: Charting the Course for Renewal

Visionary leadership can have a profound impact on a nation's development and prosperity. In Haiti's darkest moments, the power of leadership grounded in hope and divine insight can turn the tide. **Job 22:29 (KJV)** declares, "When men are cast down, then thou shalt say, There is lifting up; and he shall save the humble person." It is the responsibility of Haiti's leaders to declare this truth—to speak life and renewal into the nation.

Haiti needs leaders who understand that a nation's greatness is intricately tied to the value of its people. As **Proverbs 14:34 (NIV)** says, "Righteousness exalts a nation, but sin condemns any people." Visionary leaders must recognize and cultivate the God-given potential within their citizens, leading with integrity, courage, and a commitment to justice.

Healing the Land and Spirit

"Victory comes from finding opportunity in problems."

-Sun Tzu

The earth is not merely a physical entity; it is a divine repository of information—a living testament to the cycles of life, the choices of humanity, and the actions that shape history. It bears witness to every event, whether it be an act of justice or injustice, a moment of joy or sorrow, or an offering of love or exploitation. The earth's response to human actions is not coincidental; it is a reflection of the divine purpose imbued within it. As Rev. Chris Christian insightfully notes, "The earth is a record keeper that cares about how we relate with it." This profound perspective invites us to understand the earth not just as a vessel of resources but as a sacred entity—one that responds to our stewardship and reflects our relationship with the divine.

The Earth as a Divine Witness

The Bible speaks eloquently about the earth's role as a witness to humanity's actions. **Psalm 115:16 (NIV)** declares, "The highest heavens belong to the Lord, but the earth He has given to mankind." This verse underscores the sacred responsibility entrusted to humanity to steward and nurture the earth. The earth's reaction to human deeds is not merely physical; it is deeply spiritual. The story of Cain and Abel in **Genesis 4:9-11 (NIV)** illustrates this vividly: after Cain murdered his brother Abel, God declared, "What have you done? Listen! Your brother's blood cries out to me from the ground." This narrative reveals that the earth itself actively participates in the divine call for justice—it hears, records, and cries out against wrongdoing.

The earth has the capacity to either bless or curse its inhabitants, and this is intricately connected to how humanity honors its divine stewardship. **Hosea 2:21-22 (NIV)** speaks of a time when "the earth will respond to the grain, the new wine, and the olive oil, and they will respond to Jezreel." This harmonious exchange between earth and heaven suggests that the well-being of the earth is directly tied to the spiritual health of those who dwell upon it. When humans act in alignment with divine purpose, the earth responds with abundance; when they stray, it responds with barrenness.

Raising an Altar: A Sacred Place for Divine Encounter

To bring about true transformation in Haiti, there is a need to establish an altar—a sacred meeting place between humanity and the divine. **Jeremiah 30:20 (NIV)** contains God's promise: "Their children will be as in days of old, and their community will be established before me; I will punish all who oppress them." This promise highlights the necessity of divine protection and favor, which can only be secured through genuine spiritual engagement.

An altar is not merely a physical structure of stone or wood—it is a space of consecration, a place where divine revelation is sought and shared. Rev. Chris Christian emphasizes, "God does not deny us what He has when we genuinely share in His immortal life through submission." **Psalm 115:16 (NIV)** reminds us that the earth is given to humanity to steward and to tend, and this dominion comes with a weighty responsibility. Raising an altar is an act of stewardship, a declaration that we seek God's favor and protection over the land and its people. It is through this sacred act that a nation like Haiti can transform its reality, align itself with divine purpose, and unlock the blessings that flow from faithful stewardship.

Confronting Jezebel: The Battle Against Corrupting Influences

Jezebel is not just a historical figure—she represents the corrupting influences that exploit and subvert divine order. Known for her cunning manipulation and control over dark forces, Jezebel's presence creates a deceptive environment, blurring the lines between truth and lies, light and darkness. This influence fosters confusion, deception, and division.

The Bible warns against such corrupt influences in **Isaiah 44:25 (NIV)**, where God is described as the one "who foils the signs of false prophets and makes fools of diviners." Jezebel's tactics involve keeping people entangled in religious activities that are devoid of true spiritual significance, thereby preventing them from experiencing genuine encounters with God. Her influence is dangerous because it replaces divine revelation with mere ritualism, allowing manipulation to thrive under the guise of spirituality.

To confront and tame the influence of Jezebel, it is essential to have discernment—to see beyond the facade and recognize the forces at work. This requires a commitment to spiritual integrity, to reject all forms of deception, and to live according to divine principles. By seeking the truth of God and rejecting counterfeit spirituality, individuals and communities can overcome the corrupting forces that seek to undermine their divine purpose.

. . .

Dethrone Foreign Gods: Reclaiming Haiti's Spiritual Sovereignty

For Haiti to experience true transformation, it must confront and dismantle the influence of foreign gods and idols. The foundation of Haiti's freedom was laid by the sacrifices of its ancestors, but genuine liberation will come only when dedicated people rise to challenge these spiritual usurpers. **Psalm 50:5 (NIV)** declares, "Gather to me this consecrated people, who made a covenant with me by sacrifice." This verse underscores the power of sacrifice in establishing a renewed spiritual order.

Haiti, with its rich heritage and resilient spirit, must return to its rightful place as a beacon of strength and dignity. Every sacrificial act made in faith and devotion is a step toward reclaiming the nation's honor and purpose. Just as Jesus overcame darkness by embodying divine light, Haiti must build a new altar of life and immortality—ushering in a period of blessings and divine favor. **Exodus 20:24 (NIV)** reminds us: "Make an altar of earth for me and sacrifice on it your burnt offerings... Wherever I cause my name to be honored, I will come to you and bless you." By dethroning the idols that have held sway over the nation, Haiti can break free from spiritual chains and reclaim its divine destiny.

Drop Your Arms and Pursue Life

True transformation requires a shift in focus from conflict to constructive impact. Every community reflects the light, values, and spirit of its inhabitants. Just as Jesus brought light to Galilee, so too can individuals and communities in Haiti bring light, hope, and transformation to their environment.

Matthew 5:9 (NIV) declares, "Blessed are the peacemakers, for they will be called children of God." Peacemakers are those who embody the kingdom principles of reconciliation and renewal. In Haiti, the current state of violence and discord reflects a spiritual void—a fallen nature that needs redemption. As Rev. Chris Christian writes in his book *Be Harmless as a Dove*, "The most violent people on earth are men who continue to exist after they have lost their lives." Violence emerges from devaluation, a lack of purpose, and a spiritual emptiness. To counteract this, Haiti must cultivate environments where purpose is valued and life is celebrated—where communities are transformed by the light of God's love and the power of His Word.

Violence Sustains the Spirit of Death

The pervasive violence in Haiti is not just a symptom of social dysfunction—it is the manifestation of spiritual decay. It is the consequence of abandoning divine principles and allowing darkness to take root. **John 10:10 (NIV)** provides a powerful contrast between the forces of life and death: "The thief comes only to steal and kill and destroy; I have come that they may have life and have it to the full." Violence thrives where there is no vision, no divine purpose, and no sense of hope. To restore peace and stability, Haiti must address the spiritual roots of violence, dismantling the altars that perpetuate destruction.

Haiti's transformation will come when its people seek the light of God, rediscovering their potential and purpose. Moving beyond exploitation and embracing the path of sacrificial service and divine illumination will bring about healing for the land and secure a future of peace and prosperity.

A Divine Mandate for Healing and Restoration

Haiti stands at a crossroads, facing the opportunity to heal both its land and its people by returning to the principles of divine stewardship and spiritual renewal. The earth, as a divine repository, responds to the actions of its inhabitants, serving either as a vessel of blessings or as a conduit for consequences. By raising altars, dethroning foreign gods, pursuing peace, and confronting the roots of violence, Haiti can reclaim its divine purpose and secure a future of light and life.

The call to heal the earth of Haiti is not merely a physical endeavor but a spiritual mandate. It demands a commitment to live according to God's principles, honor the sacred trust given to humanity, and transform communities through the power of divine love and wisdom. In doing so, Haiti can fulfill its destiny as a nation under God—a beacon of hope and renewal for the entire world.

Navigating Haiti's Path to Renewal

Nobody remains the same when he has become a positive change agent

-Rev. Chris Christian

Haiti, a nation that has endured a complex and turbulent history, stands at a critical juncture today. Rich in culture and heritage, yet marred by decades of adversity, Haiti's challenges—political instability, economic hardships, and humanitarian crises—require a bold and multifaceted strategy for transformation. To usher in a new era of prosperity, Haiti must confront its past, harness its inherent strengths, and embrace a new vision. This chapter explores how Haiti can attain stability, growth, and humanitarian progress through a comprehensive approach rooted in faith, collaboration, and resilience.

Political Stability: Building the Cornerstone of Renewal

Political stability is the foundation upon which Haiti's future will be built. Without stability, progress remains an unattainable dream. Haiti must first and foremost focus on strengthening its governance and fostering inclusivity.

Revitalizing Institutions with Transparency and Accountability

To build a stable nation, Haiti must restore the strength of its governmental institutions. This requires more than just reform; it necessitates a rebirth of trust. Transparency and accountability must become the bedrock principles of public governance. Strict anti-corruption measures must be enforced, so that every Haitian knows their leaders serve not for personal gain, but for the welfare of all.

Decentralization: Empowering Communities for Local Solutions

True governance happens when power reaches the people. By decentralizing authority, Haiti can empower local communities to address their specific challenges and create tailored solutions. Local authorities who know their communities are better equipped to provide effective governance. This distribution of power can transform how services are delivered and how swiftly challenges are addressed.

Dialogue and Inclusivity: A New National Spirit

Political stability is more than the absence of conflict—it is the presence of unity. It is essential to bring every voice to the table, including marginalized groups that have long been silenced. As **Psalm 133:1 (NIV)** reminds us, "How good and pleasant it is when God's people live together in unity!" By fostering open, inclusive political dialogue, Haiti can build the national consensus needed to move forward. Civic engagement must be encouraged, and public forums must become places where the aspirations of every Haitian are heard and valued.

Upholding the Rule of Law: Justice as a Pillar of Stability

Strengthening the rule of law is not optional—it is the cornerstone of any thriving society. The independence of the judiciary must be protected and resources allocated to ensure efficiency and fairness. Only by upholding justice can the Haitian government ensure that every citizen is protected under the law, and human rights are never compromised.

Economic Development: Laying the Foundations for Prosperity

Economic development is the lifeblood of a nation seeking transformation. Haiti's economic recovery hinges on diversification, infrastructure investment, and international cooperation.

Diversifying the Economy: From Dependency to Resilience

Haiti's path to prosperity lies in economic diversification. Too long has the nation been dependent on a narrow band of industries. The future of Haiti is rich with potential—in agriculture, tourism, and manufacturing. These sectors offer tremendous opportunities for growth, job creation, and self-sufficiency. Supporting small and medium-sized enterprises (SMEs) can foster entrepreneurship and economic resilience.

Infrastructure as the Backbone of Progress

Modern infrastructure is the backbone of a thriving economy. Investments in roads, ports, and energy systems are essential for connecting Haiti's communities, facilitating trade, and attracting foreign investment. Moreover, enhancing digital infrastructure can open doors to e-commerce, online education, and remote work, integrating Haiti into the global economy and creating opportunities that were previously out of reach.

Harnessing International Partnerships for Growth

International partnerships can be a powerful catalyst for Haiti's economic revival. Strategic relationships with global organizations and nations can bring much-needed development assistance, technical expertise, and investment. As **Proverbs 21:5 (NIV)** wisely says, "The plans of the diligent lead to profit as surely as haste leads to poverty." Through diligent planning and collaboration, Haiti can turn its challenges into opportunities.

Humanitarian Progress: Cultivating Hope and Well-Being

Humanitarian progress is essential for improving the quality of life for every Haitian. To build a just and equitable society, Haiti must address poverty, inequality, and the legacy of natural disasters.

Addressing Poverty with Compassion and Support

A nation is only as strong as its most vulnerable citizens. To tackle poverty, Haiti must implement social safety nets—cash transfers, food assistance, and community support programs. By ensuring that the most vulnerable have access to education, healthcare, and clean water, Haiti can break the cycle of poverty and uplift its people. **Galatians 6:2 (NIV)** encourages us: "Carry each other's burdens, and in this way you will fulfill the law of Christ." By caring for the vulnerable, Haiti can build a foundation of compassion and solidarity.

Disaster Preparedness: Turning Vulnerability into Resilience

Haiti is no stranger to natural disasters. Earthquakes, hurricanes, and other calamities have repeatedly tested the resilience of its people. To mitigate the impact of such events, comprehensive disaster preparedness is essential. Investing in resilient infrastructure, developing early warning systems, and involving local communities in planning can make the difference between survival and devastation. When communities are prepared, they can face disasters with courage and resilience.

Championing Human Rights and Justice for All

True humanitarian progress cannot be achieved without justice. Promoting human rights—protecting children, ensuring gender equality, and supporting marginalized groups—must be central to Haiti's vision for the future. Local NGOs, faith-based organizations, and community groups are crucial partners in this mission. Their dedication to justice and equality helps create a society where everyone is valued.

A Path Forward: Crafting Haiti's New Vision

Haiti's journey to achieve stability, growth, and progress requires a vision that inspires and guides. As **Proverbs 29:18 (NIV)** states, "Where there is no vision, the people perish." A clear, strategic vision is essential for Haiti's rebirth.

Building a National Development Plan Rooted in Inclusivity

To navigate its challenges, Haiti needs a comprehensive national development plan. This plan must reflect the aspirations of every Haitian, incorporating defined goals, priorities, and timelines. It should be a beacon of hope—a plan that brings every segment of society together toward a common goal. When the marginalized are included, when every voice matters, transformation becomes possible.

. . .

Fostering Partnerships for Lasting Impact

No nation succeeds in isolation. Haiti's government, the private sector, civil society, and international allies must come together in partnership. Collaboration ensures that every resource and every effort is directed where it is needed most. As **Ecclesiastes 4:9 (NIV)** says, "Two are better than one because they have a good return for their labor." Together, Haiti can achieve what it could never achieve alone.

Guided by Faith: Persevering Through Challenges

Haiti's path is not without obstacles, but faith is its greatest ally. **Galatians 6:9 (NIV)** encourages perseverance: "Let us not become weary in doing good, for at the proper time we will reap a harvest if we do not give up." The journey may be long, but Haiti's people are resilient. They have weathered every storm, and they will rise again. With dedication, collaboration, and faith, Haiti can emerge from its challenges stronger than ever.

Navigating the Restoration of a Failed Government

Restoring a failed government requires a nuanced strategy—a combination of bold reforms, inclusive leadership, and spiritual wisdom. A failed government represents more than the absence of effective governance; it signifies a breakdown in trust, law, and public service. Haiti must take immediate, decisive actions to navigate the complexities of restoring effective governance.

Assessment and Honest Reflection

Before progress can be made, an honest assessment must be undertaken. Identifying the failures—whether corruption, economic mismanagement, or inadequate services—is crucial for devising a strategy that targets the roots of dysfunction. **Proverbs 18:13 (NIV)** reminds us, "To answer before listening—that is folly and shame." By truly understanding the problems at hand, Haiti can begin to formulate targeted solutions.

Dialogue and Reconciliation: Healing Divisions

Healing a broken government means healing the divisions within the nation. Political factions, civil society, and citizens must come together in dialogue and reconciliation. **Psalm 82:3 (NIV)** encourages us to "Defend the weak and the fatherless; uphold the cause of the poor and the oppressed." These principles remind us that governance must reflect the values of justice, compassion, and inclusivity.

Transitional Government: Restoring Trust and Order

A transitional government, representing all factions, must be established to pave the way for democratic elections. Wise leadership, as advised by Jethro to Moses in **Exodus 18:21 (NIV)**, involves selecting capable leaders of integrity. The transitional government must focus on rebuilding trust, restoring stability, and preparing for a future guided by the people's will.

Economic and Security Reforms for a Stable Future

Economic reforms, grounded in careful planning and accountability, are essential for a nation's recovery. Supporting SMEs and attracting foreign investment can create a more resilient economy. Strengthening security forces, as highlighted in **Psalm 82:3 (NIV)**, is also vital for maintaining order while respecting human rights. Reforms in security and public service delivery will be pivotal to the nation's revival.

. . .

Empowering Civil Society and Promoting Transparency

Civil society organizations play a crucial role in holding the government accountable and fostering transparency. **Proverbs 27:17 (NIV)** says, "As iron sharpens iron, so one person sharpens another." Encouraging a free and active civil society ensures that governance is constantly improving through scrutiny and constructive feedback.

Fostering Unity and Peaceful Coexistence in Haiti

Unity and peace are the twin pillars upon which a strong society stands. For Haiti, embracing these principles is essential to overcoming its current challenges.

Promoting Diversity and Inclusion

Unity is not the absence of diversity—it is the celebration of it. **Galatians 3:28 (NIV)** reminds us that "there is neither Jew nor Gentile... for you are all one in Christ Jesus." By embracing every culture, every community, and every individual, Haiti can harness the strength found in its rich diversity.

Building Healthy Relationships and Engaging Youth

Communities thrive when relationships are nurtured, and youth are engaged. **Hebrews 10:24-25 (NIV)** encourages us to "spur one another on toward love and good deeds." Engaging youth in peace-building initiatives ensures the next generation is actively shaping a society that values unity and harmony.

Leadership and Role Models: Leading by Example

Effective leadership is at the core of unity. Leaders who exemplify values of respect and inclusivity inspire others. The story of Nehemiah rebuilding the walls of Jerusalem serves as an example of leadership amidst adversity. Leaders who seek the welfare of their community can inspire transformation.

Establishing Youth Peace Platforms: A Vision for the Future

The youth of Haiti are the hope for a brighter tomorrow. Establishing platforms for young people to participate in peace initiatives is crucial for creating a lasting culture of harmony.

Youth-Led Peace Initiatives and Community Dialogues

By creating youth-led peace clubs, initiatives, and community dialogues, Haiti can cultivate the next generation of peacemakers. **Matthew 5:9 (NIV)** tells us, "Blessed are the peacemakers, for they will be called children of God." Giving youth the tools and platforms to lead peace initiatives ensures they are invested in Haiti's future.

Arts, Music, and Non-Violent Communication

Art and music are universal languages of unity. Promoting peace through creativity enables youth to express their hopes and inspire change. Non-violent communication, grounded in empathy and listening, provides the foundation for building strong relationships. **James 1:19 (NIV)** reminds us, "Everyone should be quick to listen, slow to speak, and slow to become angry."

A Divine Mandate for Renewal and Hope

Haiti stands on the threshold of change. By committing to principles of good governance, economic resilience, and humanitarian progress, Haiti can build a future that honors its past while embracing the promise of tomorrow. Guided by the wisdom of Biblical principles and practical strategies, Haiti can achieve lasting stability and prosperity.

. . .

"Two are better than one because they have a good return for their labor." (Ecclesiastes 4:9, NIV)

Haiti must embrace the power of unity, collaboration, and faith to overcome its challenges. Together, the people of Haiti can reclaim their nation's story—one of resilience, strength, and hope—and chart a course toward a future filled with promise and light.

Raising Political and Spiritual Consciousness

"Don't worry about getting old, worry about thinking old"

-Anon

Haiti, a nation of immense courage, unbreakable spirit, and an extraordinary historical legacy, stands at a pivotal moment in its journey. At this crossroads, there is a powerful need for an awakening—an elevation of both political and spiritual consciousness. These two interconnected forms of awareness, when cultivated together, possess the transformative power to unlock Haiti's potential and lead its people toward lasting renewal and progress.

Political Consciousness: Empowering a Nation for Change

Political consciousness is more than awareness; it is the power to influence change, the belief in one's role as an architect of destiny. For Haiti—a nation that has weathered a complex and often turbulent political history—awakening political consciousness is the key to building a society where every citizen takes part in shaping a better future.

Awareness: The Foundation of Political Consciousness

Political awareness begins with knowledge—knowledge of the issues that affect the nation, of government policies, and of the broader world. It requires an understanding of the structures of power and the tools available to citizens. Haiti's journey toward self-determination starts with each individual knowing their rights, their power, and their capacity to make informed choices. The Bible states in **Hosea 4:6 (NIV)**, "My people are destroyed from lack of knowledge." This verse is a profound reminder of the dangers of ignorance—of allowing misinformation, disinterest, or apathy to dictate one's future. To build a nation of empowered citizens, Haiti must prioritize education and awareness.

Political Values: Grounded in Justice and Equity

Political consciousness is also guided by values—principles such as justice, equality, and integrity. These are not abstract ideals; they are the pillars of a prosperous society. **Isaiah 1:17 (NIV)** implores us: "Learn to do right; seek justice. Defend the oppressed." In Haiti, these values must become the driving force behind every political decision, shaping a society that champions the rights of the marginalized and speaks for those whose voices have long been silenced.

Civic Engagement: The Duty of Every Haitian

Political consciousness naturally leads to action. Civic engagement—voting, attending public forums, advocating for change—is the heart of a thriving democracy. Every Haitian must understand that voting is not just a civic right; it is a moral duty to contribute to the greater good. **Proverbs 31:8-9 (NIV)** declares: "Speak up for those who cannot speak for themselves, for the rights of all who are destitute." In every vote, every protest for justice, and every call for accountability, Haitians must embrace their power to shape the future.

The Role of Media and Truth

In an age flooded with information, discerning the truth has become a critical skill. The media plays a pivotal role in shaping political consciousness, but it must be held to a standard of truth and integrity. **Proverbs 12:17 (NIV)** says, "An honest witness tells the truth, but a false witness tells lies." The people of Haiti must seek out credible sources and demand honesty, ensuring that the information guiding their political actions is rooted in fact and righteousness.

Spiritual Consciousness: The Heartbeat of Haiti

While political consciousness addresses the mechanisms of change, spiritual consciousness is about transforming the soul of the nation. It is the compass that guides decisions, the deeper calling that moves individuals to live with purpose, empathy, and a commitment to a higher good.

Awareness of the Divine: Living with Purpose

Spiritual consciousness is about recognizing a connection with the divine—a realization that every individual is part of something greater than themselves. It means aligning one's actions with values of compassion, integrity, and love. The Bible offers timeless wisdom in **Philippians 4:8 (NIV)**: "Whatever is true, whatever is noble, whatever is right, whatever is pure, whatever is lovely, whatever is admirable—if anything is excellent or praiseworthy—think about such things." By embracing this awareness, Haitians can transform their communities through acts of kindness, resilience, and hope.

. . .

Spiritual Education: Passing Down the Wisdom

Just as political consciousness grows with knowledge, spiritual consciousness flourishes through education—through learning from sacred texts, spiritual leaders, and community elders. **Deuteronomy 6:6-7 (NIV)** emphasizes the need to pass down spiritual teachings: "These commandments that I give you today are to be on your hearts. Impress them on your children." Spiritual education is the inheritance that binds generations, empowering them to face challenges with unwavering faith.

Community and Mentorship: Strengthening the Collective Spirit

Spiritual consciousness cannot thrive in isolation. It grows within the embrace of a community—through shared worship, mentorship, and mutual support. **Proverbs 27:17 (NIV)** tells us, "As iron sharpens iron, so one person sharpens another." In Haiti, spiritual leaders and mentors must rise to guide, inspire, and uplift. By fostering communities rooted in spiritual growth, Haitians can build a collective strength that becomes an unshakable foundation in times of hardship.

The Interconnected Journey: Political and Spiritual Unity

True transformation requires the harmonious interplay of both political and spiritual consciousness. Political change without spiritual grounding risks losing direction; spiritual growth without political engagement may never materialize into tangible change. Together, these forces create the momentum for a better future.

The story of Nehemiah from the Bible offers a profound example. When Nehemiah saw Jerusalem's walls in ruin, his political consciousness drove him to take action, to organize the people, and to rebuild. But it was his spiritual consciousness—his faith and prayers—that gave him the strength to overcome immense challenges (**Nehemiah 2:4-5, NIV**). Haiti needs leaders and citizens who embody this powerful blend of action and faith, of policy and prayer, to rebuild and renew the nation.

Building Grassroots Consciousness: Planting Seeds for a National Awakening

Change begins at the grassroots level, where every individual and every community plays a role in shaping the nation. Raising political and spiritual consciousness at the grassroots is about empowering communities to take ownership of their future, to realize that the power for change lies within their own hands.

Education as Empowerment

The cornerstone of grassroots consciousness is education. By providing people with the knowledge of their rights, of the issues they face, and the solutions available, communities are empowered to act. **Proverbs 4:7 (NIV)** reminds us: "The beginning of wisdom is this: Get wisdom. Though it cost all you have, get understanding." Investing in education—both political and spiritual—ensures that communities are equipped to drive change.

Community Engagement: The Strength of Collective Action

Communities thrive when people come together to address common issues, share resources, and make decisions. True progress happens when people are given a voice in the decisions that affect them. **Matthew 18:20 (NIV)** says, "For where two or three gather in my name, there am I with them." This verse speaks to the power of collective action, the strength that comes from unity. In Haiti, this kind of community engagement can transform villages and cities, making them vibrant centers of progress and hope.

· · ·

Leadership Development: Guiding the Way Forward

Leaders are not born—they are made, nurtured, and guided. Haiti needs leaders who are deeply committed to the well-being of their communities—leaders who embody integrity, humility, and resilience. **1 Timothy 3:1-7 (NIV)** provides guidance on the qualities of effective leadership. By identifying and nurturing local leaders who are willing to serve, Haiti can build a network of champions who will sustain the momentum for change at the grassroots level.

A Vision for National Transformation

The journey to raise political and spiritual consciousness in Haiti is not an easy one. It requires courage, dedication, and a willingness to confront both internal and external challenges. But it is a journey worth taking—a journey that holds the promise of a transformed nation.

A Collective Effort: United for Haiti's Future

Transforming Haiti is not the task of a single leader or organization; it is the responsibility of every Haitian. It involves a commitment to education, to engagement, and to living out spiritual principles. **Galatians 6:9 (NIV)** encourages us: "Let us not become weary in doing good, for at the proper time we will reap a harvest if we do not give up." Haiti's transformation will require perseverance, resilience, and an unshakable belief that change is possible.

Integrating Spiritual Principles into Political Action

For real change to take place, spiritual values must guide political actions. Policies must reflect the core principles of justice, compassion, and integrity. Leaders must be accountable to both their people and their Creator, recognizing that their power is a gift meant to be used for the common good. By integrating spiritual consciousness into political decision-making, Haiti can ensure that progress is not only made but sustained.

The Road to a New Haiti

Haiti is at a crossroads, but it is also at a point of opportunity—a chance to redefine its future, to rise from the ashes of its struggles, and to build a nation that is politically empowered and spiritually alive.

Political consciousness provides the tools, the knowledge, and the power to shape the external world, while spiritual consciousness offers the moral compass and the deeper purpose that guide these actions. Together, they form the foundation of a Haiti that is resilient, united, and filled with hope.

Proverbs 29:18 (NIV) says, "Where there is no vision, the people perish." Let Haiti's vision be one of justice, equity, and spiritual awakening. Let its people rise together—educated, engaged, and inspired—to create a future that honors their past and builds toward a brighter tomorrow.

Haiti's transformation is not just a dream—it is a promise. And that promise begins with each citizen, each community, and each leader raising their consciousness, standing together, and believing in the power of change. Together, Haiti can emerge as a beacon of hope, a nation reborn through the strength of its spirit and the power of its people.

ECONOMIC GROWTH AND NATION BUILDING

"Nation building is not a one-time event, but an ongoing process fueled by sustained economic growth, investment in human capital, and inclusive development."

-Unknown

Haiti—a land of immense resilience, rich cultural heritage, and unyielding hope—finds itself at a defining moment. For a nation that has faced immense socio-economic challenges and endured political instability, the prospect of economic growth and nation-building may seem elusive. Yet, beneath the surface of adversity lies an untapped well of potential waiting to be unleashed. Haiti is ready to rise again, and it is in this rise that we discover the power of unity, vision, and faith.

To transform Haiti, it is imperative to harness the nation's strengths, confront its deep-rooted challenges, and embrace a vision of economic empowerment guided by enduring principles. The promise of Haiti lies in revitalizing agriculture, leveraging cultural assets, rebuilding the manufacturing sector, and fostering righteous governance—all while grounded in timeless biblical truths.

The Agricultural Foundation: Haiti's Hidden Wealth

Haiti's history and culture are deeply rooted in the land. Agriculture is not only the lifeblood of the economy but also the key to unlocking prosperity. Nearly half of Haiti's population is involved in farming, producing significant crops like bananas, cocoa, mangoes, and vetiver oil—an essential ingredient in some of the world's finest perfumes. Yet, paradoxically, the country still imports 80% of its food, revealing a tragic underutilization of its potential.

The Bible offers a powerful vision of agricultural prosperity. **Genesis 26:12 (NIV)** tells us, "Isaac planted crops in that land and the same year reaped a hundredfold, because the Lord blessed him." Haiti, too, can reap abundance from its soil—but it requires diligent cultivation, investment, and a new perspective on its agricultural foundation. The path forward is clear: modernize agricultural practices, invest in sustainable infrastructure, empower farmers through education, and create value chains that support local production.

Imagine a Haiti where the fields are vibrant, where families prosper from the fruits of their labor, and where the country not only feeds itself but becomes a beacon of agricultural excellence in the region. With targeted investment, collaboration with agricultural experts, and the adoption of sustainable farming techniques, Haiti can break the chains of dependency, create jobs, and drive growth from the ground up.

Breaking the Chains of Debt: A Call for Justice

Haiti's economic struggles are not of its own making. They are deeply entwined with a history of exploitation and unjust debt. In 1825, France demanded an impossible "compensation" of 150 million francs for the loss of its colony, forcing Haiti into a century of economic servitude. Even as late as 1947, Haiti was still repaying this unjust debt—one that robbed generations of their rightful opportunities for growth and prosperity.

The Bible offers wisdom on debt and justice that speaks directly to Haiti's plight. **Proverbs 22:7 (NIV)** warns, "The rich rule over the poor, and the borrower is slave to the lender." Haiti's struggle against the weight of debt has been a testament to this truth—a nation shackled by obligations imposed upon it by foreign powers. Today, the call for reparations and the acknowledgment of past wrongs is more than symbolic; it is a moral imperative. True economic freedom for Haiti requires not just debt forgiveness but the establishment of equitable relationships and investment in its future.

To break free from this historical burden, Haiti must advocate for global partnerships based on justice and equality. The international community has a responsibility to support Haiti not through charity, but by righting historical wrongs—through reparations, investment, and fair trade agreements that empower rather than exploit.

Rising from the Rubble: Building Resilience in the Face of Disasters

Haiti's vulnerability to natural disasters has tested its people's resilience time and again. The 2010 earthquake, one of the most devastating in modern history, claimed countless lives and left deep scars that remain to this day. Despite the challenges, Haiti's spirit remains unbroken. The rebuilding process has been slow, and international aid has often fallen short of addressing the root causes of vulnerability.

Psalm 46:1-3 (NIV) offers comfort in times of devastation: "God is our refuge and strength, an ever-present help in trouble. Therefore, we will not fear, though the earth gives way and the mountains fall into the heart of the sea." This passage speaks directly to Haiti's journey—a journey of finding strength in the face of unimaginable loss. For Haiti to truly rebuild, it must embrace resilience not only in its infrastructure but in the hearts and minds of its people.

This means constructing buildings that can withstand natural forces, developing early warning systems, and empowering communities to be prepared for future disasters. Resilience is not just about physical structures; it is about cultivating hope, unity, and preparedness—ensuring that every Haitian is part of the nation's renewal. By investing in disaster-resistant infrastructure and community-led preparedness programs, Haiti can transform its vulnerability into strength, creating a safer and more stable foundation for growth.

Righteous Leadership: The Cornerstone of Nation Building

No nation can prosper without strong, righteous leadership. Haiti has suffered from political instability—frequent changes in government, corruption, and the lack of visionary leadership have impeded the nation's progress. For true nation-building, Haiti needs leaders who serve the people with integrity, transparency, and a commitment to justice.

Proverbs 29:2 (NIV) speaks clearly on this matter: "When the righteous thrive, the people rejoice; when the wicked rule, the people groan." Haiti's people are yearning for leaders who will put their interests first, who will uplift rather than exploit, and who will build rather than destroy. It is time for a new generation of leaders to rise—leaders who are accountable to both God and the people they serve.

These leaders must prioritize education, healthcare, infrastructure, and job creation. They must foster an environment where businesses can flourish, where farmers are supported, and where every Haitian can see a path to prosperity. Only through righteous governance can Haiti establish the foundation necessary for sustained economic growth, social stability, and national pride.

. . .

A Vision for Haiti's Future: Prosperity Through Unity and Action

Haiti's journey toward economic growth and nation-building is undoubtedly fraught with challenges, but it is also rich with opportunity. By embracing a holistic approach—one that honors the past while boldly stepping into the future—Haiti can rise again.

1. **Agricultural Renaissance**: Haiti must see agriculture not as a relic of the past, but as the backbone of its future. By modernizing farming practices, supporting local farmers, and fostering innovation, Haiti can transform agriculture into a source of national pride and economic power.

2. **Manufacturing and Cultural Industries**: Beyond agriculture, Haiti's manufacturing sector holds untapped potential. The nation's rich cultural heritage —its art, music, and craftsmanship—can be harnessed to create jobs, attract tourism, and position Haiti as a hub of creativity. By investing in local artisans, building manufacturing capacity, and creating a brand that reflects Haiti's unique identity, the nation can diversify its economy and uplift its people.

3. **Equitable Global Partnerships**: The time has come for Haiti to forge new relationships with the international community—relationships based on mutual respect, justice, and opportunity. Reparations for historical injustices, fair trade agreements, and investment in Haiti's infrastructure are essential to creating an environment where the nation can thrive independently.

4. **Disaster Resilience and Preparedness**: Haiti must become a model of resilience in the face of natural disasters. By investing in disaster-resistant infrastructure, empowering communities, and fostering a culture of preparedness, Haiti can reduce the impact

of future events and create a safer environment for its citizens.

5. **Leadership Rooted in Integrity**: The cornerstone of Haiti's future is righteous leadership—leaders who govern with humility, who prioritize the well-being of their people, and who lead by example. These leaders must cultivate a culture of accountability, transparency, and service.

Hope for a Nation Reborn

The story of Haiti is not one of despair; it is a story of hope, resilience, and the power of the human spirit. It is a story of a people who, despite centuries of challenges, have never given up on their dream of freedom, prosperity, and peace. The journey ahead is not easy, but it is filled with promise. Guided by principles of justice, resilience, and righteous governance, Haiti has the opportunity to rise as a beacon of hope—a testament to what is possible when a nation commits itself to growth and renewal.

Isaiah 61:4 (NIV) declares, "They will rebuild the ancient ruins and restore the places long devastated; they will renew the ruined cities that have been devastated for generations." Haiti's path to economic growth and nation-building is a journey of rebuilding, of restoring what has been lost, and of renewing a spirit that has endured through centuries of struggle.

It is time for Haiti to reclaim its story, to rise from the challenges of the past, and to build a future that reflects the strength, beauty, and potential of its people. With faith, unity, and a shared vision, Haiti can achieve economic growth and become a thriving nation—a land reborn, blessed, and prosperous.

A New Model for Recovery

"Effective governance is not about control from the top; it is about creating transparent systems that allow every voice to be heard and every action to be accountable."

-Philip W. Mshelia

In the heart of the Caribbean, Haiti—a nation of resilience, culture, and untapped potential—stands at a crossroads. The country has faced wave after wave of challenges, from natural disasters and economic hardship to political instability and social inequality. The Haiti Renewal and Resilience Initiative (HRRI) aims to break the cycle and ignite a profound transformation. HRRI offers a comprehensive, community-driven blueprint to shape Haiti's progress through resilience, empowerment, and a spirit of unity. The initiative is grounded in four key pillars: Humanitarian Relief, Social Empowerment, Spiritual Renewal, and Governance Reform—each inspired by successful global models and guided by sustainable, community-focused innovation.

. . .

1. Humanitarian Relief and Development: Building Resilience from Within

Humanitarian relief and long-term development must go hand-in-hand if Haiti is to build true resilience against the disasters that have defined much of its modern history. HRRI seeks to turn vulnerability into strength, drawing inspiration from global successes such as Rwanda's community-driven reforms.

Integrated Humanitarian Relief Teams

The HRRI's approach is holistic, built on the successes of Rwanda's National Disaster Management Authority (NDMA) and the coordination seen in global responses like the Humanitarian OpenStreetMap Team. Haiti will have multidisciplinary relief teams equipped with medical professionals, engineers, data analysts, and logisticians—all working with real-time data to predict disasters and respond with precision. Leveraging technology like Microsoft's COVID-19 Data Lake, these teams will prioritize local capacity-building, empowering communities to take charge of their own futures.

Imagine the transformation when every community in Haiti has its own local disaster team equipped and ready—residents who know the land, anticipate risks, and respond effectively, rather than waiting for foreign aid.

Community-Based Disaster Risk Reduction (CBDRR)

Inspired by Rwanda's Ubudehe System, which empowers communities to categorize themselves based on vulnerability and resilience needs, HRRI introduces a "Disaster Resilience Index" for Haiti. This Index allows communities to assess, prepare for, and mitigate disaster risks with targeted, community-specific interventions. It's about local ownership—where community members are not merely recipients of aid, but active architects of their own safety and security.

. . .

Sustainable Livelihood Programs

To reduce Haiti's food dependency, HRRI introduces innovative Agri-Tech Solutions such as hydroponics and vertical farming, much like Israel's transformative agricultural initiatives. Coupled with Haiti's traditional agricultural practices and inspired by Rwanda's Land Husbandry, Water Harvesting, and Hillside Irrigation project, the focus is on nurturing sustainable farming practices that not only feed the nation but create surplus for export, positioning Haiti as an agricultural hub in the Caribbean.

Clean Water and Sanitation Campaigns

Access to clean water is a foundation of public health. HRRI draws inspiration from Singapore's NEWater Initiative, integrating water recycling and rainwater harvesting into communities. By coupling Rwanda's Community Health Club model, which focuses on hygiene education, with innovative technology, Haiti can significantly reduce waterborne diseases and give every community the dignity of clean water—a right, not a privilege.

2. Social Empowerment and Inclusion: Building Haiti's Human Capital

Haiti's progress relies on its people—especially its youth and marginalized communities. HRRI places a premium on empowering every Haitian through education, economic opportunities, and equitable access to resources, inspired by Rwanda's inclusive development model.

Community Schools and Education Hubs

HRRI will establish Blended Learning Community Hubs, equipped with offline digital platforms like Khan Academy and

Duolingo. Following Rwanda's One Laptop per Child (OLPC) initiative, Haiti will empower its youth with digital literacy, vocational training, and entrepreneurship skills. These hubs will bridge the digital divide, making education accessible to all, and providing skills that directly lead to employment and community development.

Youth Leadership and Peace-Building Programs

Inspired by Rwanda's National Youth Council and drawing on the Escuela Nueva Model, HRRI will launch youth leadership programs focused on civic engagement and entrepreneurship. Imagine Haitian youth equipped with tools from Generation Unlimited, leading their communities out of poverty, resolving conflicts, and spearheading innovation. The goal is to transform Haiti's most promising generation into agents of change—an unstoppable force for social progress.

Women's Empowerment Initiatives

HRRI recognizes the key role of women in Haiti's development. Inspired by Rwanda's National Gender Policy and Ghana's AIDA Digital Platform, HRRI will provide women with mobile tools for financial literacy, entrepreneurship, and health. By empowering women economically and socially, HRRI aims to foster an environment where women are central to decision-making processes, economic growth, and community well-being.

Community Media and Information Centers

Building on Bolivia's Community Radio Network model, HRRI will bring Mobile Radio Stations and Podcast Platforms to even the remotest parts of Haiti. Trained community journalists will use mobile tools to report on local governance, educate the public, and hold leaders accountable, fostering transparency and civic participation that is truly grassroots.

3. Spiritual Renewal and Cultural Revitalization: Reclaiming Haiti's Soul

Haiti's cultural and spiritual heritage is its strength, a source of resilience and pride. HRRI integrates faith, culture, and environmental stewardship into a holistic renewal process that draws on Rwanda's successful reconciliation and cultural preservation initiatives.

Faith-Based Community Healing Programs

Post-trauma recovery is about healing the spirit as much as the body. Inspired by Rwanda's HROC (Healing and Rebuilding Our Communities) model, HRRI will collaborate with local churches, vodou practitioners, and interfaith groups to offer trauma recovery through mindfulness and spirituality. Haiti's rich tapestry of faith traditions will be woven into a nationwide healing journey—one that acknowledges past pain while building hope for the future.

Cultural Heritage and Arts Revival Centers

Revitalizing Haiti's cultural pride is a critical part of nation-building. HRRI will establish Cultural Heritage and Arts Revival Centers that draw inspiration from Brazil's AfroReggae and Rwanda's Ingando Re-Education Camps. By incorporating platforms like Scratch, Haitian youth will learn coding and digital arts to celebrate their heritage through storytelling and creative expression—making Haiti not just a country with a history, but a nation with a future.

Moral and Ethical Leadership Forums

HRRI will establish Leadership Incubators inspired by Rwanda's Itorero Leadership Academy. These incubators will equip emerging leaders with courses on ethics, governance, and leadership —using a combination of online platforms and immersive face-to-face workshops. The goal is to nurture leaders who lead with vision and integrity, inspired by the biblical call to righteous governance.

Spiritual and Environmental Stewardship Programs

Drawing from Ethiopia's Green Legacy Initiative and Kenya's Green Belt Movement, HRRI will lead Faith-Led Reforestation Campaigns, engaging local faith communities in environmental stewardship. This echoes Rwanda's Umuganda, a community clean-up and preservation initiative—rooting sustainability in both cultural values and spiritual duty.

4. Governance Reform and Civic Engagement: Laying the Foundation for Stability

True nation-building requires transparent and inclusive governance. HRRI's approach to governance draws heavily on Rwanda's experience, emphasizing community participation, accountability, and ethical leadership.

Decentralized Local Governance Model

HRRI will introduce Digital Citizen Engagement Platforms inspired by Estonia's e-Estonia Platform and Rwanda's Imihigo system, allowing citizens to engage in decision-making, report issues, and track government performance online. Local governance will be strengthened, and service delivery made more accountable—all within the reach of every Haitian citizen.

Citizen-Led Monitoring and Accountability Platforms

Building on Kenya's Uwiano Platform, HRRI will use

blockchain technology for real-time monitoring of public services, enabling transparency and minimizing corruption. This empowers Haitians to hold their leaders accountable—not with protests or violence, but with data and technology that ensures integrity.

National Integrity and Anti-Corruption Campaigns

Inspired by Georgia's Anti-Corruption Bureau, HRRI will employ AI and machine learning to detect corruption patterns. Rwanda's success as one of Africa's least corrupt countries serves as an inspiration for Haiti, proving that change is possible with rigorous oversight and innovative tools.

Electoral Reform and Civic Education Programs

HRRI will use Virtual Reality (VR) to create immersive civic education experiences, engaging youth in understanding democratic processes and the importance of fair elections. Modeled after Rwanda's voter education initiatives, this approach aims to foster informed, active participation among Haiti's future leaders.

Resilience and Governance Training for Local Leaders

Leveraging the training models of Singapore's Civil Service College and Rwanda's Local Government Academy, HRRI will offer ongoing education to local leaders. The focus is on crisis management, governance, and ethics—ensuring that leadership is capable, accountable, and responsive to the needs of all Haitians.

The HRRI Vision: A New Dawn for Haiti

The Haiti Renewal and Resilience Initiative (HRRI) is more than a recovery plan—it is a vision of a thriving, resilient Haiti, a nation empowered by its people, grounded in its cultural and spiritual identity, and led by ethical governance. By embracing global best practices and tailoring them to Haiti's unique context, HRRI seeks to create a sustainable path to inclusive growth, resilience, and prosperity.

Imagine a Haiti where communities are self-reliant in disaster preparedness, where education hubs empower the youth, where faith and culture are celebrated and used as pillars for nation-building, and where governance is transparent, inclusive, and just. HRRI embodies a paradigm shift—from dependency to empowerment, from fragility to resilience, from stagnation to growth.

Proverbs 29:18 (NIV) tells us, "Where there is no vision, the people perish." HRRI is the vision that Haiti needs—a roadmap to rebuild not just the economy, but the spirit of the nation. It is an invitation for the world to witness what true resilience looks like, crafted not by foreign hands alone but driven by the people of Haiti, with their indomitable will, their rich traditions, and their enduring hope.

It is time for Haiti to be more than a symbol of struggle. It is time for Haiti to become a beacon of what is possible—a testament to the strength of a people who, against all odds, chose renewal, resilience, and hope.

MANIFESTATION OF HAITI

"When the time is right, I, the Lord, will make it happen."

- Isaiah 60:22 (NLT)

In a world where nations rise and fall, where power and influence shift with time, there is a higher calling for countries that look beyond wealth, beyond dominance. It is the calling to shine a light in the darkness, to be a beacon that inspires not only its people but the world at large. Haiti, a nation long perceived as downtrodden, is on the brink of an extraordinary awakening—a manifestation destined to elevate it as a beacon of hope and progress for the Caribbean and for the world.

Haiti's Prophetic Destiny: Rising with the Spirit of Africa

Haiti's destiny is intertwined with a greater prophetic vision—the rise of Africa and her children in this millennium. This era marks a divine shift, an awakening of nations once oppressed, now rising in honor and influence. Haiti, with her rich African heritage, shares in this sacred calling. This connection is not coincidental; it is purposeful, a sign of the interconnected destinies of Africa and Haiti. As Africa rises, Haiti is also poised to stand tall, breaking the chains of her past and stepping into a future of boundless promise.

This moment demands that the people of Haiti lift their eyes beyond the horizon of their struggles and see themselves through the lens of their true potential. They are not abandoned, not forgotten, but chosen for greatness. Haiti is not destined to be a symbol of perpetual suffering, but rather, an emblem of resilience and rebirth. Even those who may not acknowledge the presence of a higher power cannot deny the spiritual essence that pulses through the history of this land. Haiti's journey from darkness to light is a testament to the presence of a divine force—a journey that proclaims to the world that hope, redemption, and triumph are within reach.

The Albatross of the Caribbean: A Metaphor of Resilience and Grace

Haiti is the Albatross of the Caribbean, a symbol of endurance, strength, and unyielding spirit. The albatross, a majestic bird, soars across vast oceans, unbothered by the fiercest storms, propelled by an unbreakable connection to the forces of nature. In the same way, Haiti has navigated storm after storm—colonial oppression, political unrest, natural calamities—each one forging a deeper resilience, a more profound grace. It is this resilience that makes Haiti exceptional, capable of soaring higher despite the winds of adversity.

The albatross is not deterred by distance or tempest. It travels vast distances with unwavering grace, traversing the unknown, sustained by an inner strength and a purpose that cannot be denied. Haiti, too, is driven by an unbreakable spirit—an energy nurtured through centuries of struggle, a determination that no amount of hardship could extinguish. In every challenge, Haiti found the seeds of strength. In every obstacle, Haiti discovered its power to overcome.

Like the albatross returning home after a long, solitary journey to give birth to new life, Haiti now stands at the threshold of a new era, ready to give birth to hope, prosperity, and unity. The past, marked by hardship and trial, has not been in vain. It has laid a foundation—a fertile ground upon which a new Haiti is rising, a Haiti that will be celebrated not for the weight of her burdens but for the power of her resilience and her ability to transcend.

Igniting the Light of Hope: Haiti's Future Begins Now

The manifestation of Haiti as a beacon of hope and progress is not just a dream—it is a reality that is unfolding before our eyes. Haiti is reclaiming her identity, embracing her destiny, and rewriting her narrative. No longer is this a story of despair; it is a story of rebirth, where the trials of the past become the fuel for the triumphs of tomorrow.

Haiti's light is not just for her people; it is for the world to witness, to be inspired, and to be transformed. This light represents the resilience of the human spirit, the unyielding power of hope, and the truth that even in the darkest night, the dawn will always break. Haiti's journey is a living testament to the belief that there is always a way forward—no matter the circumstances, no matter the challenges.

As Haiti moves forward, she carries with her the strength of her ancestors, the wisdom forged through struggle, and the promise of a future filled with possibility. This is a future where Haiti rises not only as a nation of endurance but as a leader—a beacon that guides others through their own storms. The albatross no longer symbolizes burden; it symbolizes grace, freedom, and limitless potential.

A Call to the World: Witness the Power of Transformation

Haiti's rise is not only a triumph for its people; it is a message to the world. In this new millennium, where the quest for progress often overlooks the essence of humanity, Haiti stands as a reminder of what true greatness looks like. Greatness is not about material wealth or political power; it is about the spirit, the heart, and the indomitable will to rise. Haiti's story is one of transformation—from survival to triumph, from darkness to light—a transformation that can inspire and uplift all of humanity.

The world must now look to Haiti and see the potential that lies within every challenge. Haiti's manifestation as a beacon of hope and progress is a call to action for every individual, every community, every nation. It is a call to recognize that progress comes not through division, but through unity; not through power, but through compassion. "Blessed are the peacemakers, for they shall be called sons of God" (Matthew 5:9). Haiti's journey is a call to peace, to unity, and to the realization that the greatest achievements come when people come together for a shared purpose, driven by hope.

Manifesting Haiti: A Vision of Progress and Unity

Let the world turn its eyes to Haiti, the Albatross of the Caribbean, and find inspiration to soar to new heights. Let Haiti's transformation be a beacon that shines through the darkness, illuminating the power of resilience, hope, and unity. In Haiti's rise, we witness something extraordinary: the triumph of a people who refused to be broken, who embraced their identity and turned their struggles into strengths.

The manifestation of Haiti is not just about rebuilding a nation —it is about igniting a movement. It is about transforming mindsets, elevating communities, and creating a new paradigm of progress that is defined by human dignity, love, and possibility. Haiti is emerging as a leader, not because of wealth or political influence, but because of her heart, her courage, and her unyielding spirit.

As we watch this nation rise, let us also find the courage within ourselves to rise. Let Haiti remind us all that no matter where we come from, no matter the obstacles we face, we have the power to manifest greatness. The dawn is breaking over Haiti, and the light is spreading—offering hope to every corner of the world. Haiti's story is a powerful testament that nothing is impossible. It shows us that, with unity, vision, and unwavering belief, even the most broken places can become beacons of hope and progress.

"And let us not grow weary in doing good, for in due season we will reap, if we do not give up."

- Galatians 6:9

Haiti is reaping the rewards of resilience. Let us join in her journey and make our own lives, communities, and nations reflect the same unyielding hope and promise. Together, we can witness the manifestation of Haiti as a beacon—a shining example that, no matter how fierce the storm, we all have the power to rise, to heal, and to soar.

Bibliography

- AfroReggae (2016). Social Impact Report.
- BRAC (2020). Annual Report.
- CRS (2018). Community Radio and Social Change in Bolivia.
- FAO (2020). Ethiopia's Green Legacy Initiative: Progress Report.
- IEC (2018). Facilitating Democracy in South Africa.
- Lee Kuan Yew School of Public Policy (2021). Governance Excellence: Singapore's Experience.
- Oxford Research Group (2019). Moral Re-Armament in Africa: A Path to Ethical Leadership.
- Rwanda Governance Board (2020). Local Governance in Rwanda: A Decade of Success.
- Rwanda Reconciliation Barometer (2021). Healing and Rebuilding Our Communities: Impact Assessment.
- SEWA (2019). Women's Empowerment: SEWA's Achievements.
- Transparency International (2019). Anti-Corruption Reforms in Georgia: A Case Study.
- UNDP (2011). Haiti Earthquake Recovery Report.
- UNDP (2015). Uwiano Platform for Peace: Monitoring and Reporting.
- UNESCO (2018). Community-Based Education in El Salvador: Lessons from Educo.
- UNDRR (2020). Localizing Disaster Risk Reduction: The Barangay Experience.
- WaterAid (2017). Community Health Clubs in Rwanda: Reducing Waterborne Diseases.
- WHO (2016). Ebola Outbreak Response in West Africa: A Review.
- World Bank (2013). Youth Engagement in Colombia: The Escuela Nueva Model.
- World Bank (2021). Poverty Data: Haiti.
- World Economic Forum (2022). Digital Inclusion and Innovation in Agriculture.